VIEWPOINT

poetry Pt today

VIEWPOINT OF A POET

Edited by
Rebecca Mee

First published in Great Britain in 1999 by Poetry
Today, an imprint of
Penhaligon Page Ltd, 12 Godric Square, Maxwell Road,
Peterborough. PE2 7JJ

© Copyright Contributors 1999

All rights reserved. No part of this publication may be
reproduced, stored in a retrieval system, or transmitted
in any form or by any means, without prior permission
from the author(s).

A Catalogue record for this book is available from the
British Library

ISBN 1 86226 512 7

Typesetting and layout, Penhaligon Page Ltd, England.
Printed and bound by Forward Press Ltd, England

Foreword

Viewpoint Of A Poet is a compilation of poetry, featuring some of our finest poets. The book gives an insight into the essence of modern living and deals with the reality of life today. We think we have created an anthology with a universal appeal.

There are many technical aspects to the writing of poetry and *Viewpoint Of A Poet* contains free verse and examples of more structured work from a wealth of talented poets.

Poetry is a coat of many colours. Today's poets write in a limitless array of styles: traditional rhyming poetry is as alive and kicking today as modern free-verse. Language ranges from easily accessible to intricate and elusive.

Poems have a lot to offer in our fast-paced 'instant' world. Reading poems gives us an opportunity to sit back and explore ourselves and the world around us.

Contents

Glory Of Christmas	Norma Christina Robson	1
Winter's End	Jim Petrie	2
Upon Reflection	M A Phillips	3
Vita Nuova	Beryl Louise Penny	4
Images In October	Peter Howarth	5
A July Day	Sheila Seabourne	7
Spring Now Reigns	Rosalind Lowe	8
The Old Moon	Jacqueline Jones	9
Seaweed's Gown	Emma Scott-Cook	10
Winter	Pauline Davison	12
Ode To Winter	J Bradford	13
The Slide	Kenneth C Steven	14
Prelude To Eternal Winter	Lucy K Ferguson	15
Another Spring	Ken Merry	16
Now In Autumn	Brian Corns	17
September	Jean Greenall	18
Spring Rides	E M Schorb	19
Summertide	Michael Monaghan	20
English Heat	Heather Aspinall	22
A Cradle Song	Tom Clarke	23
The Last Day Of August	Janet Sellars	24
Morning	K Iles	25
As Spring Is Walking In	Emma Williams	26
First Snow Of Winter	Margaret Revill	27
Winter Fun	Patrick T Brady	28
Wind	Chris White	30
Down By The Seashore	Malcolm Wilson Bucknall	31
Reflective Thought	Freda Ringrose	32
Summer	William Holmes	33
Hallowe'en	Shirley Frances Winskill	35
The Spirit Of Christmas Past	Mot Nosbod	36
A Winter's Day	Nora M Kirienko	37
Flower Of Christmas	Teresa Jeanne Smith	38
Sou'wester	John Nolan	39
Christmas	J Boast	41

The Wind	Vicki Turner	42
Winter Song	Barbara Fosh	43
Frost	Josephine Haden	45
Moonlight	K B Osborne	46
Thoughts Of Winter	Pauline Brown	47
April	Hazel Maiden	49
The Christmas Fairy	Kay Carr	50
Autumn	P M Jay	51
An August Day	T L Baldwin	52
Storm On Malham Moor	Frank Littlewood	53
Changing Season	Pam Ismail	54
Flash	David Batten	55
Hallowe'en	Ivy Boyne	56
Happiness Was Everywhere	Claire Hughes	57
Tidal	Nora M Davidson	59
Adieu	Neil A Forrester	60
The Pot And The Kettle	John Cunningham	61
November	Struan Yule	62
Birds Of The Seasons	Elsie Francis Yeatman	63
Fantasies	Joan Tompkins	64
Autumn	P A Ilott	66
Spring	Yvonne King	67
On A Cold Winter's Day	Christina Jarrett	68
Autumn Trees	Jessica Davies	69
Christmas Cheer	Peter Edward Waines Briggs	70
Season's Delights	Margaret M Osoba	71
Twilight	Pat Westland	72
Fireworks	Kate Hensher	73
A Sunshower	D Futer	74
Watching The Weather	Barbara Coward	75
Spring Is Waiting	Jan Sewell	76
A Little Easter Song	Patricia Sköld	77
The Christmas Cracker	Jim Pritchard	78
Four Seasons Of Life	Barbara Morrow	80
Children In Dreams	Kenneth Mark Alla	81
The True Christmas Spirit	Christine Bolton-Pearson	82
Rainbows	Marty Greenwell	84
Autumn	Jennifer C Taylor	85

Memories	Carolyn Finch	86
Leaves	Fiona Higgins	87
Season Of Goodwill	Hazel Smith	88
Another Year Goes By	Lawrence Joseph Sparks	89
Untitled	M Connor	90
Autumn	Valerie J Owen	91
The Storm	Nancy Knight	92
A Happy Wholesome Christmas	Rosemary Peach	93
An Autumn Morning	D Williams	95
Winter's Wind	Katie Hill	96
The Skies Have It	D G Viall	97
Autumn Fairies	Beryl Smyter	98
Awakening	Daisy Thompson	99
An Ode For A Summer Love	Mike Achiampong	100
Winter	Stan Tweedie	101
Kid's Christmas	Joan Plant	102
A Summer Corn Field	D Godbold	103
The Battlefield	Nina du Pille	104
Forgotten Fleets Reunion (Portsmouth 1995)	Bill Scovell	105
Untitled	B Manfredi	106
Weather Forecast	Philip Tyler	107
Impatience	I M Parker	108
Circle Of Life	Marion Moylan	109
Last Wolf	Stuart Grant	110
The Immigrant	Margaret Mary Hurley	111
Phenomenon	P Ashby	112
Garden Of Delight	Jon Wilde	113

Glory Of Christmas

Ice encrusted pools of darkness
Nestling in the frost rimed earth
Brittle-bright between the branches
Hangs the sun, a new day's birth.

O'er the fields the cattle lowing
Echoes on the frosty air,
Christmas is once more before us
In a stable, lowly there -

Born to us a child, our Saviour,
Son of God so meek and mild,
Humbly now we kneel before him,
Jesus Christ the Holy Child.

Angel Voices sweetly singing
Proudly tell of Jesus' birth,
Through the night their anthem ringing
'Peace to men, - Goodwill on earth.'

Norma Christina Robson

Winter's End

Grey-green swords in clusters
pierce the tan-brown earth.
Rain falls in sleety flurries,
a fire glows in the hearth.
Leftover leaves from autumn
swirl round in the gusting wind
dead branches from the old oak tree
lie broken on the ground.

Spring isn't far away, they say
in the pub and club and shop.
The winter hasn't been too bad
the snows forgotten, once they stop.
A summer like the last, is what
they're asking for again
but they will moan about the heat
and the parched grass, needing rain.

A Niagara Falls of rain water
falling from the leaf-choked rone,
remind the happy optimist
that winter is not yet gone.
The forecast is for snow and frost
and cold winds from the east
so the grey-green shoots of the daffodil
may be early, to say the least.

Jim Petrie

Upon Reflection

When a child, Christmas never comes;
In middle years time runs in a spate
Of remembered longing
And thoughtful apprehension.

But the year that is now
Is always the best time;
The bad times are those
That seem worse, upon reflection.

M A Phillips

Vita Nuova

Grey robes of Winter clothe the earth
Faded Autumn's splendour
The swallows fly to lands of sun and ease
Over the lonely seas
The leafless hedgerow, bare of Summer's richness
Braves the icy blast,
The woodland creatures in their fastness
Slumber deep. The night-black crow
Is toss'd in darkling skies by the frolic winds.

And when the sun appears
All nature wakes to warmth and light,
The seeded wheat in the fields springing green,
A smiling primrose peeps from leafy crown,
The flickering sunbeams spread warm caress
As people dream, in hope of Summer days,
And drifts of snowdrops shine in woodland ways,
The dawn brings in the birdsongs with their praise,
Welcome to the bright new year! New life has begun.

Beryl Louise Penny

Images In October

The sun and gold in earnest due
To hamlets squat and quiet in frost
Lifts the spell of night and spreads the morning hue
Until the black is lost,
When braids of fog around
The shoulders mountainous bare
Drift off without a sound
Through the chilly expectant air.
The sounds of life will soon return
In gold and green and blue.

The sinuous track rises into the hazy blue
Of High Crag, imposing, and there
Reposes in silence as the martin flew,
Encircling the fells in the icy air.
A lonely climber rests, looking where
His climb had come from way below,
From the distant, palest hue.
Across the mirrored fells his eyes passed o'er
And the beauty shrined in golden awe
Before his taste, and nature began unfurling.
But he reached into his heart-felt core
Of questions, love and inner feeling,
And found his heart was home, his mind at rest,
The clarity of truth and the beauty of reason blessed.

What silent rings the raindrops formed
In the window silvered clear
Here and there, until bestormed
By a shower, thence to disappear
Into the confluence of the waves.
The shadows darkened, then danced away
Lost in the depths of watery graves
As the water turned a steely, dusky grey.
The rain conceals the face of the morn
And the cold wind sweeps and shivers
Along the fells and paths forlorn,
Across all the lakes and rivers.
But the character of the land shone through
With every cadence of subtlety and hue.

Peter Howarth

A July Day

I would wrap this day up and store away
Until a dull November day,
Then, unwind each memory one by one.

First, the golden July sun,
Burnished garden, cool shady trees,
Roses, Mallows, alive with bees.
Grandchildren chattering, wine and pasta,
The day devoured, faster and faster.
Tea on the lawn, the shadows lengthening.
One golden day, the family strengthening.

Wrap each piece, carefully, carefully,
Store in the mind, gently, gently.
Old age will come, children then gone.
No sorrow will dim this July sun.

    Sheila Seabourne

Spring Now Reigns

Winter has fled, the spring now reigns
and warming sunlight brings to life the earth
that once was stark and barren - life within it comatoze
but now is full of bright re-birth.

See, at our feet, with dazzling rays
the gem-like crocus hails the joyous morn'!
Exquisite gold and purple blooms
make carnival-like the jaded earth
once so forlorn.

Rosalind Lowe

The Old Moon

The old moon is a fabled shape
Under which ancient clichés rock and break,
But look closer and it has been tainted,
By touch of finger, by one who painted
On the glass, a dankness of obscure it
To relic of dust, chalk, memory and pit.
A planet burnt out long ago,
Fills the giant hall of hollow.

The moon is as frightening as a skull,
The owl who dreams it, slowly makes a cull.
The moon is a crisp statement now,
A distant and ruthless orb of snow.

Witness how it dissolves under the fingers
Of dawn creeping sabered dangers.
The day is its absolute undoing,
But by the sun, it remains shadowing,

In the scales of our human loving.

Jacqueline Jones

Seaweed's Gown

Silken, her dress swirls through like the gossamer sea.
Stiff, and brave within its wetted firmament, she
Clutches, coldly, the weathered edges of its shroud.

Engrossed in love's pale veils, and keen,
Her suitor waits with raw soliloquies.
Conscious, barely, of the seagull's weedy yelp
And hearing, high, the plaintive murmur of her churchy lips.

The pew-people, watch with lidded eyes
As their breath, bated, clouds that weathered edifice.
They seek, blindly, the echo
Which is caved deeper than the heart's whimper.

He thinks
Of the ethereal cottage on the cliff.
Of its far-off threshold
Twinkling like a horizon of stars.

She thinks
Of the bitter tide of love.
And of her mother, who also swirled
Beneath these arches and configurations.

A blue-bride.
A blue-bride -
Who, leaving her beloved and her quiet child,
Walked so strange into the sea's strange arms.

Something borrowed, he says.
Something blue, she replies.

Something
Like the sea's bright eye.

   Emma Scott-Cook

Winter

Winter, stark and creeping,
A chill wind blowing,
The daylight hours short.
Night comes too soon.
Cold and endless dark
Brings no flowers
To brighten long hours
Borne in twilight.
Yet the crimson skies
Of sunrise and sunset,
Their scarlet hues
Delight my eyes.

Pauline Davison

Ode To Winter

Autumnal voices whisper that the end is nigh,
Trees in forests so deep have shed their withered leaves,
Harvests are gathered, frosty breath and a gentle sigh,
Who let bleak Winter in - its mystery has begun to weave.

Damp evenings seem darker, gone is the light -
Encased in a cocoon - I fear the cold.
The silvery moon shines bright, what a wondrous sight!
Casting shadows that flicker, for its tales it must unfold.

The first snowflakes fall on a carpet so meek and bare -
Rosy hues reflecting through gnarled and twisted arms
Of branches that strain as crisp snow lies everywhere,
With nature switching to dormant - 'tis a scene so very calm.

Short days go by and a white blanket has formed,
I'm touched by your spell, my dear Jack Frost.
Breathe unto me, for what you unveil is adorned,
When embedded in snow, the earth beneath you appears lost.

With a glimmer of hope for nature surviving hibernation,
Strength and determination bring seeds of warmer days -
A new world awakes from a long spell - such joy and elation,
The colour of Spring is upon us - Winter vanishing in a phase.

J Bradford

The Slide

We longed for the sharp crinkle of December stars,
That ghostly mist like cobwebs in the grass -
Ten degrees below zero.

After the snow came petalling from the skies,
Settled into a deep quilt, the frost
Diamonded the top, making a thick crust.

On the long descent of the lawn
We made our slide, planed the ground
Hour after hour till it smiled like ice.

At night we teetered out with buckets,
Rushed the water down the slide's length
In one black stain.

Next day the slide was lethal,
A curling glacier that shot us downhill
In a single hiss.

Even after the thaw greened our world again
The slide remained written in the grass
As long as our stories.

Kenneth C Steven

Prelude To Eternal Winter

As the sun slides up and over the endless horizon
The moon yawns and quietly slips away,
No sound can be heard, except the awakenings of a new day.

You lie there, as if asleep, your eyes closed,
Forever peaceful, forever more,
But where you lie the sun cannot reach,
Its spindly grasp cannot thaw the hard ice that surrounds you.

You lie there in the dark alone, waiting for that tiny fragment of
                                                            life,
Yet it will never come.
There in the winter of darkness where the sun never rises
And the questions remain unasked,
You will stay.

   Lucy K Ferguson

Another Spring

Another spring
and you are alive
and distant from pain.
Through visiting rain
another spring
will promise to give
the sun's returning.
Although slow burning
it will bring
the power active
to drive back again
the north's cold domain.

Ken Merry

Now In Autumn

There are no nightingales now in autumn,
the swallows unremarked have gone,
there is only now the driving west wind,
gusting rain, and growing dark.
    Yet even now the sun in the morning
    early is bright and gently warm,
    and in the hedges late flowers blossom
    while blackberries fill, ripen and fall.

Brian Corns

September

I still wonder at the beauty
In the pellucid light of a mid-September day,
Postponing the fall of darker days.
Still sparkling sun on honeysuckle berries
Garnet glow 'midst sparse remaining blossom.
Dragonflies dance as if full summer still
And blackberries glisten - some fully ripe
Luscious bursting bounty to gather
Whilst red unripe fruit lie,
Under protecting nettles sharply
Stinging the unwary.

Jean Greenall

Spring Rides

It is like this now at the end of winter.
The poor trees have survived, like
the poor blacks and the poor whites
along the highway, who wave as you fly by.
They have survived another long winter.

Now surpose someone in a passing car,
someone very rich, were to heave from the car
a suitcase filled with money,
then in spring the trees would spend it
on new clothes and the little girls
would be wearing fresh leaves and flowers
on a breezy church day and would look 'like a million' -
Well, there you have the waiting trees with their tight buds.

It is like that now at the beginning of warmth.
I have been waiting, like a willow for the wind,
hanging loose but useless, for the busy world outside,
though I have run my leagues and burned my wheels
waiting for winter to haul out - for here is not Aspen
down the slopes but a pickup stuck in a bog -
and now my drive is full of Flowering Judas,
and older today I feel younger than yesterday
and for no real reason am convinced of tomorrow.

    E M Schorb

Summertide

Arising one morning I shook my weary head; rays of golden
                               sunshine revolved about my bed,
Opening up the windows to allow fresh air into the room;
I was greeted by the fragrance of my garden flowers perfumes;
In looking towards the garden wall, my red roses I could see being
pollinated thoroughly by swarms of flighty bumble bees,
In the heavens above that were coloured blue, the swifts and
                               swallows rapidly flew, soaring
across the open fields they plucked countless midges for their meals,
After breakfast I left my country home, outward to the coast I had
                                     decided to roam,

On arrival the tides were out, with a mass of screaming
                               people running all about,
'Ice-cream! Ice-cream!' A vendor did yell 'It's a beautiful day,
                                   I've got plenty to sell!'
The crowds thronged around the vendor like bees around honey, one
child shrieked, 'I lost all me money!'
When all the hue and cry passed away, money being found,
                 everyone was smiling, no face had a frown,

Walking along the sands I witnessed kites flying with multitudes of
people on the ground mostly lying,
Some bodies were eating cheese and partaking of wine, they didn't
seem to notice when I asked them the time,
Into the madness of this magnificent day saneness I did seek,
Phew! The smell of the seaweed oh! How it did reek!

Women, I observed, wore straw hats, while their menfolk and children were digging holes like rats,
Further along the open shore there were countless sandcastles, a hundred or more,
Beach-brollies, deckchairs everywhere, beachballs travelling through the air,
Sudden shouts of glee in my ear did sound from bathers who had turned from white to brown,
These sunworshipers then ran into the sea until incoming waters washed over their knees,
Observance once more before I was homeward bound, I recollected memories of this day I had found,
Birds, bees, blue skies and seas, folk sunbathing wherever they pleased,

Water now splashing over my burning feet, I accepted it gratefully as the season's cooling treat,
Yearning for home lapsed in daydream, the ghost of my countryside pub stood before me there,
The landlord he invited me to sit down on my usual chair,
In wiping sweat from my forehead I longed for a cool beer, to raise my glass with him on this day of good cheer,
Finally, I wanted to proclaim a toast to all who sat near,
'Here's to you glorious Summer at last you are here!'

Michael Monaghan

English Heat

Now sit and think of summer breeze
Air so fresh and warm
Joyful faces of passers-by
Looking forward the forgotten storm
Summer heat! But are things so sweet?
When beneath this dress of happiness
Lies a deeper message of summer madness.

Too many people seem to forget
That the companionship of the sun
Can itself be a threat!
Not unlike bees to a flower
People congregate in bars
And after drinking far too much
Many drive home in their cars!

A combination of alcohol and sun
Not only temperatures run high!
When a sunny afternoon drink can end
With a glass in someone's eye!
Love call it lust also rises with heat
Whistles proposition people
While they are walking down the street.

Heather Aspinall

A Cradle Song

A boy was born at Christmas time,
all young and soft and fair.
His mother held him closely by,
with tender loving care.

No bells rang out to greet the morn,
no trumpets did proclaim;
but all around the people stood,
for Jesus was his name.

A star shone bright in Bethlehem,
across the silent sky
and in her arms now fast asleep,
a new born King did lie.

Three Wisemen came with special gifts,
to see the humble sight;
for heaven had sent new hope to man,
in one small babe that night.

Tom Clarke

The Last Day Of August

It was very hot.
England baked under a heatwave.
The lucky ones - with time off -
Flocked to the sea,
Desperate for even a slight breeze.
We found a beach with not so many people.
A black dog was jumping in and out of a small boat
Grounded in the wet sand.
We put our shoes side by side on the pebbles,
You turned up your trouser legs,
And we paddled - moving slowly from sandy patch to sandy
                                                                            patch -
While the ocean took one deep breath after another,
Gathered momentum,
And rolled and tumbled the waves onto our bare legs
Before disappearing into the shingle.
The wet tide mark moved higher up the coloured pebbles
And the foam drained back - ready for the next time.
A small family established itself in deckchairs near the shell-
                                                                               line.
The children gathered and sorted with excitement.
The parents watched the children.
And the grandmother watched us.
We stood knee-deep in the sea,
Laughing at my hat, holding it when it lifted in the thin wind,
Enjoying the waves breaking all around us.

   Janet Sellars

Morning

Early morning is the time
For all the birds to sing,
And nature is a lovely rhyme,
It's then your heart takes wing
And soars above the world at rest
In peaceful slumber still,
And revels in the wind's caress
Then falls upon a hill.
As, from the top, you view the scene
Of beauty stretched before you
You know, at last, just what it means
To have someone adore you.
For love is like the early morn,
It beautifies the soul,
And then you know that you were born
To give your love to all.
A love to friend, a love to foe,
A love to everyone you know,
But more than this, you know is true
A love to all those who love you.

K Iles

As Spring Is Walking In

As spring is walking in, the daffodils
start to blossom.
The little buds start popping open, the
flowers get to work.
Snowdrops trying to break the soil,
and the tree buds tightly sealed
crispy leaves are set aside.
For spring is walking in - the dawn
of a new year is just beginning!

Emma Williams (10)

First Snow Of Winter

White,
Pure white,
Drifts down,
Covers all around.
White,
Pure light,
Shining all around.
Changes this dismal place
Into pure enchantment.
Makes a dream world come
Into my mind.
Makes reality fade.
Come dance with me -
A new tune we shall find.
All evil covered,
All sins hidden,
Until the thaw -
All is forgiven.

    Margaret Revill

Winter Fun

Sat alone,
not for long.

Starin' at a manky wheel trim
drinkin', smokin',
the Scream in the background.

I can see
see the wind blowin',
winter's a comin'
Comin' with a fuckin' vengeance.

I have a theory,
true, or not. I don't know.
You have a good summer,
you get a cunt of a winter.

This morning I saw
the first so called flake,
flake of snow.
Winter is here!

She's speaking but
I'm not really listenin',
I'm thinking,
thinking about winter.

Three layers of clothes,
four pairs of socks,
and wet woolly gloves.

Tryin' to make a good snowball,
with freezing fingers,
in wet woolly gloves.

This is what I call
Winter Fun.

Patrick T Brady

Wind

is a tangled sea like a thought's
        undergrowth. I have
loitered above those milky orts

many times and in the knots seen
        the sinew and bone
of the forest. And in the keen

autumn sky many clouds have raced
        as they race today -
shifting gleams where my thoughts are traced,

liquid as all the treetops are -
        fully-thrust thought, tinge
of the gold-veined word, and afar

calm as at the heart of the bay.

    Chris White

Down By The Seashore

Down by the seashore - morning's silence -
  Is fractured by the seabird's cries,
As - like feathered ghosts they flutter -
  From the cold dark sombre skies.

On the wet sands - scarred by shingle.
Seagulls squawk 'spasmodically' -
As they strut. Amongst. The debris -
Thrown up by the angered sea.

Secure in clefts on - craggy rock face -
Seabirds view the lonely beach, - as
In the dark skies - full of anguish.
Their echoed cries - drift out of reach.

   Malcolm Wilson Bucknall

Reflective Thought

The sun shines down brightly in happiest mood,
Capping wet hair in safe, warm, snood.
That same sun skimming a calm blue sea,
As I sit on the beach,
With clasped hands on knee.
Waves lapping silently, slowly, in studied repose -
Gently caressing my warm bare toes.

I sit and savour this moment in time,
Rippling waves edging the sand so fine.
And thus I sit quietly in sheer delight,
As the warm sun and sea wait to welcome the night!

Freda Ringrose

Summer

How nice to go walking,
On warm, hazy summer days,
To come upon those leafy
And shady country lanes.

Where sweet and fragrant air
Assails your tired face
Thus bidding you to slow
Your city quickened pace.

To drink in and survey,
All the beauty
Of these golden,
Sunny days.

To store mental note of
All the sights and sounds,
The distant mournful baying
Of country nurtured hounds.

The soporific humming of the Bee
The gentle song of nearby Stream
The distant whirr of Dragonfly
The staccato calls of Crows in sky!

The hard rutted furrows,
Last winters now sun-baked mud,
Cows drowsing in the pasture,
Contented, chewing cud!

Sweetly scented grasses
And freshly mown-down hays,
Convey all the pleasure,
Of these lovely sun-soaked days.

These things we can remember
Safely keep and store
To comfort us in winter when
November's wind blows once more.

   William Holmes

Hallowe'en

This is the night of threatening doom
        When Witches Fly;
When shadows flicker across the room,
        And Spirits spy:
And magic hangs heavy upon the air,
And the sly, old fox forsakes his lair,
And strange cats prowl, with eyes that glare,
And the bullfrog croaks, 'Beware, Beware!'
        And Witches Fly!

This is the night when Evil glows,
        When Witches Fly;
When the old, stone fountain overflows,
        And Owlets cry:
And wizards chant their secret rune,
And black shapes hover around the moon,
And the night air moans a wild, wild tune,
And Hecate stirs the cauldron's spoon,
        And Witches Fly!

   Shirley Frances Winskill

The Spirit Of Christmas Past

I remember, of days long past
the heavy curtains, to keep out the blast
of ice cold air in unheated rooms,
stone hot-water bottles, frosty moons,
whose bright white glow reveals a scene,
of cart rutted snow and vaseline,
used to rub on wind chapped thighs,
the smell of piping hot mince pies.
The gas lamp hiss and frozen breaths
and miniature steam engines, run on meths.
Of paper-rounds in sleet slanting rain,
then thawing fingers, racked with pain.
Of queuing with mum at 'Palmer Hall',
collecting the 'divi' that provides our All,
at Christmas time, a time of joy,
at least, it was, for one young boy.
It really was magic, my memory tells.
Santa Claus and Jingle Bells,
pillowcased presents, a cork popping gun,
and silence, from the chicken run.
I thought then it lasted, just one day.
How wrong I was; *'It's here to stay'*

Mot Nosbod

A Winter's Day

What is more lovely than a winter's day?
The earth lies still beneath the palest grey
Of heaven, and granite rock and fallen leaf
Know no man's foot.
The river quietly licks the ice-clad stone,
The faintest whisper tells of where it runs,
And throws the trees their image in a pool
That even fish deserted long ago.
The silence can be heard and seen and felt
Of all things known, that lie beneath the snow.

Nora M Kirienko

Flower Of Christmas

White and graceful
Like the lily,
Purer than the icy snow,
Grows the lovely flower of Christmas,
Rosa Rose de la Noël.

Touched with silver
By the moonbeams,
Gilded by the noon-day sun,
Stands the glorious flower of Christmas,
Rosa Rose de la Noël.

Flowers that bloom
In salutation
Of our God who gave His son,
Grows the only flower of Christmas,
Rosa Rose de la Noël.

Petals touched with
Rainbow prisms
From the Star of Bethlehem,
Stands the purist flower of Christmas,
Rosa Rose de la Noël.

Guarding watching
Tiny Jesus
On His very day of birth,
Mary named it Rose of Christmas,
Rosa Rose de la Noël.

Teresa Jeanne Smith

Sou'wester

Blowing through from Lundy
Along the Severn shore
Curling white the wave-tops
Sullen, angry roar

Echoed o'er the marshes
Lonely seagull cry
By the storm wind driven
Across a glowering sky

Shrilling in the marsh grass
Tearing at the clumps
Of stunted blackthorn bushes
And fattened cattle rumps

Grumbling in the chimneys
Slashing icy rain
O'er each shining roof slate
Every windowpane

In the marshland hamlets
Braced against the blast
By flickering firelight's shadows
Burnished patterns cast

Brimming full the field dyke
Lashing branches bare
Racing always inland
Rampant, without care

Boisterous sou'wester
Would that I could be
Rid of man's false fetters
Wild, untamed as thee

John Nolan

Christmas

When we hear the bells on Christmas day
It seems as if they want to say
'Greetings to all, this wondrous morn
Give thanks for the day when Christ was born
Peace and joy we pray for you
Not just today, but all year through.'

J Boast

The Wind

The wind unseen blows where it will,
Sometimes loud and rough, seldom quiet and still.
It can bend whole trees or rustle a leaf.
It can pass through woods like a stealthy thief.

It has many names and different forms,
Breeze, gale, hurricane the force behind storms.
It can raise white horses or high Atlantic seas.
It can ruffle your hair or push you to your knees.

The wind that fills the billowing sails
Is the same that twitches the animals tails.
It gently lifts a child's paper kite
Or tosses an aeroplane with its might.

Wind causes the ripened fruit to fall
Shouts with piercing whistle or howling call.
It stops our breath or makes us gasp.
It can tug things easily from our grasp.

It can bend our backs and drives the rain
Travelling as fast as an express train.
Gently it cools us when the sun is high,
Refreshing us with a gentle sigh.

Vicki Turner

Winter Song

On a winter's scene
When peering out
It makes you think
What's life about?

The birds still brightly
Sing their song
Though winds blow bitter
And snow lasts long.

They know the gardens
Where they'll find bread
Seem to tell each other
I wonder what's said?

Lined up on rooftops
Way up high
They don't miss a thing
That passes by.

Like a feathered army
All face the same way
'Eyes right,' 'Eyes left'
They seem to say!

Then all of a sudden
I know not why
They all decide together
To fly up to the sky!

They swoop and they swerve
In a most graceful way
Settle down on a tree
To ponder and stay.

Then one gets bored
And leaves the rest
I wonder if he's gone
Back to his nest?

The twilight comes
The sun goes down
All is silent
All around -
Except perhaps for a twitter.

Barbara Fosh

Frost

A night for magic!

The moon,
heaven-hung in velvet vastness,
shot the world with wonder,
and shadows crouched like beasts
about to spring.
Silhouettes of trees -
dark against darkness.
Levelled lawn and limpid lake,
bordered bush-black.

> Singing silence,
> like a spell of enchantment,
> threaded thought with wonder.

Unseen, unheard, he wrought his magic:
breathing upon windows,
touching trees with twisting fingers
(leaves shrinking from his cold caress).
Slinking through grasses,
sprinkling them with silver dust;
threading slyly through still waters,
leaving them stiff and numb with horror.

> But with the morn
> reluctantly acceding to the sun,
> withdrawing into shadows, there to wait
> for yet another night.

Josephine Haden

Moonlight

Oh silver moon how cold you look suspended in the sky
Watching over all the world from way up on high.
Sending down your silver beams to play upon the sea
And lighting up both hill and dell and every bush and tree.
Oh small friendly silver ball lighting up my way.
You are free to everyone forever and a day.

K B Osborne

Thoughts Of Winter

Clouds above us, clouds below,
Layer upon layer of drifted snow.
Bare the trees now, branches clashing,
Empty nests - wild winds dashing.

Frost-painted pictures on windowpanes,
Season of red noses, pain of chilblains,
Water frozen on lake and river
Children sliding, sledging - joyful ever

A pale sun gleams on weathervanes
Snowball fights in streets and lanes
Hushed is the traffic in the town
As flakes like feathers come drifting down

Rain, hail, sleet and snow
Buffet the earth and all below;
Wonder of wonders, look at the trees
In the garden with their lace-like frieze.

Icicles like crystal against the wall
Are the most wonderful sight of all,
'Neath a cover of snow the earth is at rest
Waiting to burgeon at spring's behest.

Howling gales and pouring rain,
Fields lie fallow 'neath a snowy counterpane,
Storm-tossed birds, seeking their rest,
A red sun sinking in the west.

Robins now are begging their bread,
Those merry little minstrels with their breasts of red,
Cattle warm in their winter byre,
Mistletoe, holly and the Yuletide fire.

Pauline Brown

April

Promise of summer scents the breeze
Warm air clings to yet bare trees
April joy is here at last
Winter gloom has gone and passed.

Birds call the mating game
Beautiful songs, happy refrain
Ladybirds like living jewels
Adorn the flowers, grasses and pools.

Baby animals and humans breathe
April's magic is surely weaved
Count your blessings, now's the time
And think of summer days divine.

Hazel Maiden

The Christmas Fairy

Count the days to Christmas, cross them off one by one,
If only it was simple, the same for everyone.
Some will have a good time, for some it will be poor,
Is the sorrow never ending? Must it be for evermore?

Can the Angel keep on smiling from the glitter on the tree,
Is she really happy? The way she looks to you and me.
Is her sad heart breaking as all below unfurls,
Or does she see a ray of hope for the children of the world?

She looks down on wondrous scenes of happiness and joy,
A family together, for every child a toy.
But secretly she hears the agonising call
Of children who are hungry and her silent teardrops fall.

But still the Angel hopes for better days ahead,
When children everywhere lie safe and warm in bed.
The world may show compassion, give help to those in need,
Do away with selfishness, banish all the greed.

The children pack the Angel away until next year,
She knows that she is safe, needs nothing, has no fear.
Her faith in all humanity with help from up above
Sends her smiling once again, to wait, with hope and love.

Kay Carr

Autumn

Patterns on the pavement
Where sun and breezes play
Hide and seek with crisping leaves
All on an autumn day.
Nature's putting on a show
Of colour and fine blooms.
Look what I can do, she says,
To keep winter at bay.
Clear blue skies and sweet fresh air.
Autumn days beyond compare.

   P M Jay

An August Day

The sun rose above the horizon in a blaze of violent reds.
Etched below the little clouds sailing in a space of blue.
The wind not much to speak of came up from the south that
                                                                    morn.

The sun blazed down in glory from a sky criss crossed by planes.
Spreading their vapour to show us where they had come from
Their direction is all we can gather to say where those trails will
                                                                     end.

Running around on the school field. Its grass dry and burnt a
                                          light brown.
Two traffic cones used as the goalposts for children to practice
                                          their skills
Of trapping the ball and then passing and shooting at goal near
                                          and far.

The sky becomes cloudy and heavy. The temperature increases
                                          each hour.
A mass of dark clouds spreads beneath it and the wind holds its
                                          breath as it waits
For the pitta patta of raindrops and the rumble of thunder from
                                          high

The paddling pool is full and inviting. All splashing and shouts of
                                          the play
The wind blows in eddies expectant as the air loses heat for the
                                          day.
And we say goodbye to today's summer with the flash of the
                                          lightning at play.

T L Baldwin

Storm On Malham Moor

The thick and heavy threatening cloud lies low
On Malham Moor, obscuring in its shades
The lime-scar heights, releasing great cascades
Of angry tumbling water, turgid flow
That sweeping through the heather turns each stream
Into a towering torrent. Every rill
Becomes a waterfall, to splash and spill
Down rocky rain-soaked slopes, a peat-stained cream,
Forming at its feet a swirling lake
That fills the river beds, and washing deep
Across the roads forms dangerous floods that keep
The anxious driver stamping on his brake;
A hostile scene, yet in its awesome way
As grand as than that on any summer's day.

Frank Littlewood

Changing Season

That olde oak tree stood naked and bare;
A skeleton now in the autumn air:
Stripped of all its summer glory.
The leaves were shed like sequences
Of that story.
A season's chapters fluttered from their branches.
A swirling wind whisked the tale
In frenzied dances.
Separating the will in atmospheric trances.
Shedding foliage to the earth below.
Foliage withers on the ground.
The will resembles into autumn's crown.
Summer's sovereignty fades away;
Until another day
When revival's story comes interplay.

Pam Ismail

Flash

Dread daffodils, we weep to see
        You back again so soon
The moment you have died away
We're on the way to June
        Hey! Hey!
It's Wimbledon again -
Boat Race, Cup Final done
Then Derby, all the Tests, and oh!
The year's well on the run

It's but a flash, like Bonfire Night
        And then Remembrance day
Advent, and Christmas on our hands
        The New Year on its way
        Too soon
Our year is getting old, as we
        Hey-Ho!
What can poor mortals do
Dear daffodils? One thing we can't -
        We cannot welcome you

(With apologies to Robert Herrick)

    David Batten

Hallowe'en

Where were you on that night of nights
When I sailed through the stars above?
I searched each part of the velvet black
But could not find you love.
I looked on the moon but had no luck.
A rocket flew by and I had to duck
I stopped at each twinkling star to see
If you were waiting there for me,
I even searched, for what it's worth
Down upon this sad old earth.
But I got my cloak caught on a thistle,
Then I lost from my broom a bristle.
Then I fell over my old black cat.
Lost a shooting star from my hat.
I thought I'd conjure up a spell,
But even that didn't go too well
I got my cauldron stuck in a bog.
And all I conjured up was a frog.
So I thought it best if I flew back.
Up to the stars in the inky black
A bit dishevelled, and worse for wear.
But still I could not find you there.
I asked around each witch I knew.
But still no good, they hadn't seen you.
So where were you on that night of nights
When most things went wrong, and little went right
When I searched for you in the stars above.
Where were you, my love, my love?

Ivy Boyne

Happiness Was Everywhere

Happiness was everywhere
The garden filled with flowers
It was although Mother Nature
Was using all her powers.

The wind was blowing, the trees swaying
The world full of bliss
Everything stood out
There was nothing you could miss.

Birds flew around
Trying to make a nest
And each and everyone of them
Wanted theirs to be the best.

Everything was joyful
The lambs sprung with glee
And somewhere nearby
Was the constant humming of a bee.

Everything sparkled
In the morning dew
Everything shone
As though it was new.

The frogs hopped about
In and out their pond
Everything was held together
By a special bond.

The sun shone a golden light
Spilling all its rays,
There has never been such a lovely morn
Never in all the world's days.

This day was a perfect day
And it will always be in our mind
As the loveliest day in history
That you will ever find.

Claire Hughes (11)

Tidal

Ebb and flow
Tide,
Our journey guide,
Waves a-rippling
Blue and bright,
Hurtling spray throwing
Rainbow light,
Boats and eider
Waves obey,
In their creator trust.
Steadfast
In harmonious toil
Till target reached:
So
Father of earth and
Heaven,
Like them
On our
Life's wave,
In your soul
Brave
All our lives of
Ebb and flow

Nora M Davidson

Adieu

My friend lay still, was almost gone,
Towards his final sleep,
His eyes like drops of water shone,
The light reflecting deep.

How many days we'd run afar,
Through woods of leafy green,
O'er shingle white and sandy bar,
A flaming sunset seen.

My chum, my pal, you're fading fast,
Your eyes are rimmed with fog,
Your loyal heart is stilled at last,
My dear old faithful dog.

Neil A Forrester

The Pot And The Kettle

I had a vision of a shepherd,
he was holding a white stick,
his sheep were wearing shades,
and their coats were rather thick.

In the distance there was an abattoir,
the shepherd wore a jester's hat,
he was singing aloud, with a swing in his walk,
but his notes were rather flat.

The sheep were strangely quiet,
I think they knew what was to come,
as they gained ground on the abattoir,
I could hear the preacher's gun.

Surely there was more of a reason,
for this shepherd to fatten his sheep,
it didn't make sense just to kill them,
after watching over them, week after week.

And on the sheep went behind him
a sign read *Welcome*, at the door,
No need for a contribution,
No need for your life no more.

Outside the abattoir,
stood a young boy crying,
he held his head in his hands,
In my father's house,
he said onto me,
The devil is taking command.

John Cunningham

November

The silver-coated bark of hillside birch
enshrouded by a leafy cloak of gold
will offer full protection and a perch
for garden finches seeking a safe hold.

But nebulous November makes obscure
precisely when the jaundiced leaves will fall;
yet in good time not one remains secure;
the birch, once Midas-touched, is shorn of all.

Its rod-like arms spell out in semaphore
a welcome to the redwing refugees
from Scandinavia fiorded shore,
sub-zero temperatured and snowbound trees.

The mavises and blackbirds entertain
their migrant cousins while they here remain.

Struan Yule

Birds Of The Seasons

I heard a cuckoo call!
Felt the sunlight caress my face
A new dawn - another life
Eager anticipation of the year to come
Heady bluebells carpet woodland glades,
Their pungent aroma fills the air.
A blackbird sings!
Wild notes in the wind
Like droplets from a summer shower
Whispering breezes - white beaches - tranquil waters
Happy days of sun-kissed meadows.
Balmy nights of velvety darkness.
Swallows glide in cloudless skies
On wings outstretched to reach the heavens
Soaring - drifting - soon to fly to faraway shores
Lazy mellow days - melancholy days of autumn.
Now the robin - pert and cheeky - breast puffed out
Against cruel winter winds.
Snowflakes swirl in haunting silence.
Blue carpets exchanged for a blanket of white.
Soundless - sleeping - all is peaceful
Waiting for the call of spring.

Elsie Francis Yeatman

Fantasies

In a drifting cloud relax
Let its vapours drape
Round your contours as you watch
Its ever-changing shape.

Glide upon a gentle breeze
Wheresoever it blows.
Feel its power in your bones
As its vapour grows.

Sail within a snowflake's breast
Curl yourself up tight.
There you'll see how snowflakes dance
In their headlong flight.

Hover on a skylark's wing
Soar within its note.
Far above the lofty trees
Watch its trembling throat.

To a rainbow's splendid arch
Down a sunbeam plane,
There to witness unseen hands
Painting drops of rain.

Ride upon a honey bee
Clasp its tiny form
Down among the dark brown hairs
Where it's nice and warm.

Look around a bee's domain
See inside a comb.
Watch a queen bee and her brood
In their cosy home.

Cruise upon a fallling leaf
Staying, if you dare,
While your trembling craft performs
Manoeuvres in the air.

On a downy feather float
By the water's edge.
Watch the baby ducklings play
In and out the sedge.

Never let your brain stagnate
Let it wander free.
Where the hand of Nature plays,
That's the place to be.

Joan Tompkins

Autumn

Although 'tis sad to see the end,
    of glorious summer days.
Utter not a word against,
    the following autumnal ways.
The wind doth blow and it may snow,
    leaving you with red faces.
Underneath the ground there lies,
    a host of dormant species.
Many of them cannot be born,
    until the spring is here.
Now how are they to do that?
    If autumn doth not appear.

P A Ilott

Spring

Folk talk about springtime, but what does it mean?
It used to be when the first flowers were seen
Now some seem to bloom all the year round,
Even daisies on lawns under snow can be found
Spring used to be gentle the rain light and warm
Now when it rains it's usually a storm.
The weather is changing it's gone quite berserk
None of the old sayings now seem to work.
A red sky at night you'd smile 'cos you knew
You would wake up to sunshine and skies of blue.
A bright starry night meant dry with a frost
Not anymore, believe that at your cost.
You've no sooner counted the stars in the plough
When you feel heavy raindrops fall on your brow.
It's so unpredictable we just never know
If we'll get sunshine, rain fog or snow.
It must be confusing for the flowers and the trees
Not only them the birds and the bees.
A few days of sunshine they wake up with zest
Time for birds to start building a nest
P'raps not just yet, there's frost in the air
Might even snow but that would be rare.
They all seem to cope, why should we complain?
Whoops: where's my brolly it's raining again.

Yvonne King

On A Cold Winter's Day

On a frosty day
Where bare trees lay and kids play
Fun is all around

But snow is still falling
Go! Have fun but do not run
Don't! Walk on the pond
Snow is melting away
It gets warmer everyday
Just a little longer.

The steamy winds blow
We might still have snow. Ho! Ho!
Creamy snow like wool.

Christina Jarrett (9)

Autumn Trees

Ancient beeches on the hill
tall, majestic still,
softly drift your golden leaves
upon the breeze.

Your magic essence will enfold
all those who pass beneath your gold,
and tread this carpet rich and fair
of fallen leaves,
upon the pathway there.
Wayfarer, stand awhile with me
lost in the beauty of a golden tree.

Jessica Davies

Christmas Cheer

I love to hear the singing
When Christmas time is here
The sound of church bells ringing
The people full of cheer
The excitement of the children
Waiting for Santa, on his sleigh
Wondering what he'll bring them
When he comes, on Christmas day
Listening to carols, sung, by a local choir
Preparing, the traditional turkey
Roasting chestnuts, by the fire
A tree, all lit with fairy lights
The holly and mistletoe
The decorations, hung, just right
Casting shadows, in the fire's glow
The presents, around the Christmas tree
Mince pies, a glass of wine
Waiting for Christmas day, to see
Which presents are theirs
Which ones are mine.

Peter Edward Waines Briggs

Season's Delights

Lammikin, lammikin, fill up your pannikin,
        Gather the briar
        To build up the fire.
See how the water so merrily bubbles.
        Put tea in the pan.
        It's all ready, Gran. -
Oh, a picnic in summer's the greatest of feasts.

Lammikin, lammikin, nights have grown dark again.
        Winter is here
        With frost cold and clear.
Draw close the curtains - all snug and warm.
        Marshmallow toasts,
        Tales about ghosts
And pictures in fireflames - oh, winter's such fun!

    Margaret M Osoba

Twilight

The greying hill fades in the rising mist,
The sky darkens, night is almost come.
A blackbird, finishing his evening song, falls into silence.
The trees sway, dipping their branches, as the gentle wind
Whispers a night-song,
Breathing the blessing of a summer night,
While in the twilight the drowsy world
Falls quietly asleep.

Pat Westland

Fireworks

Bonfire night
Not quite.
But even so that doesn't stop
The fizz, bang, whiz
Of money going up in smoke.

Against this multi-coloured
Star-spangled backdrop
In the DIY carpark
TEXAS, illuminated, tries to compete.
Basic, practical, functional
Do-it-yourself
And forsaking all others
We light the heap
Of touches, glances, whispers
That have amassed between us.

Suddenly, all the crashing, thundering, exploding
Rockets overhead, have got nothing
On that first kiss, that leaves me
A Katherine wheel.
Dizzy, spinning,
Sparkling, reeling.

Separate cars, separate homes
Both of us
Not thinking, only feeling,
While the flame speeds up the touch paper.
Burning
       Dangerously
               Explosively.

Kate Hensher

A Sunshower

A sudden shower of rain poured down, out from the sunlit sky,
Falling from a large dark cloud, which slowly drifted by.
The teaming rain in the bright sunlight, shone like silver streams.
A shining rainbow lit the sky, like a magic fairy scene.

The passing cloud just drifted by, on a light south western breeze
And darkened shadows filtered past, and dulled the bright
                                                                  green trees.
The rain poured down, the puddles formed, upon the ground
                                                                         below,
Then in the sky, a chink of light, the sun again began to show.

The rainstreams glinted in their fall, like crystals once again,
And soft green leaves upon the trees, shed the drops of falling
                                                                           rain.
The darkened cloud was drifting off, afar across the sky.
And sunbeams now poured down again, and soon around all
                                                                    would be dry.

The rainbow faded in the light, the sky was clear and blue,
The earth and trees were now refreshed, everything looked new.
The fairy scene was over now, life settled down again,
We know now what a sunshower is, sunshine mixed with falling
                                                                           rain.

D Futer

Watching The Weather

The wind is really howling outside
And the weathermen forecast gales countrywide
The clouds are racing across the sky
Outrunning an aeroplane flying by.

Now the rain is battering down
Beating its rhythm against hard solid ground
Swelling the puddles, rivers and streams
Till they become too full and burst at the seams.

Look, the sun has finally come out
Trying its hardest to dry and warm all about
But on the horizon once more rain clouds appear
Speeding across the sky with such revelry.

It's vibrant, it's forceful this turbulent weather
As rain, wind and sun all get together
A part of nature that cannot be ruled
All one can do is to watch - entralled!

Barbara Coward

Spring Is Waiting

Silver-mirrored, the sea lies placid,
basking in the clear cold sunlight.
No boats bob and dip.
They sleep late this early spring morning.

Colours spice the brown earth
as dainty daffodils
drink in the unaccustomed warmth.
Small green shoots
shyly peep from naked branches,
promising a verdant future.

A gentle laughter fills the air
as strangers-warmly clad -
raise weathered faces to the beaming sun.

Smiling exchanges - a sharing.
Spring brings new life and hope.
This moment - captured -
Forever a memory
To ward away the darkness of the night.

Jan Sewell

A Little Easter Song

Oh, awake, you happy throng,
Easter comes with thanks and song.
Hear the lark's trill on the wing,
Joyful warbling in the spring.
All creation pours out praise
And our longing hearts we raise.
   Oh, God, our Creator!

See the cross upon the hill!
It is empty now, but will
Always speak a message clear,
Take away our shame and fear.
For Christ's victory o'er the grave
Gives us hope, our souls to save.
   Oh, Jesus our Saviour!

Feast our eyes upon the flowers!
Lilies fair and leafy bowers,
Daffodils and lilacs sweet -
All unite our Lord to greet.
See the little lambs at play
Innocent, this joyous day.
   Oh, Jesus, Lamb of God!

One day in the morning bright
On our souls will dawn a light
And our tears be wiped away,
On that great and wondrous day,
And all cleansed from sin and shame.
In His presence praise His name.
   Oh, Jesus, forever. Amen.

Patricia Sköld

The Christmas Cracker

Christmas comes but once a year, twice we could not take -
with all the things that must be bought to boil or roast or bake.
Of course there must be presents, but really on *'The Day'* -
it's the good old Christmas dinner that takes pride of place, I say.

There's all the preparation, some done the day before,
but still the cooking to be done - suggest you start at four.
If this you do then gradually the meals all cooked and hot,
just think it only took ten hours to feed this flaming lot.

So, down you sit and drink the health of all the friends you know,
include the postman, milkman too, no - not him - his cow.
There is much more to Christmas than toasting all you meet,
Of course there is the Chef calls in,
'Just shift yourselves - Let's Eat.'

Before you even eat a crumb there's one thing we hold dear,
it's cracker pulling time once more - it comes round every year.
The crackers pop and hats fly out, with mottos - some quite rude,
and then come presents at a pace, and land right in the food.

There are motor cars and animals and prehistoric sheep,
then puzzles, cubes and 'no name things'-
enough to make you weep.
The plastic toy that never works, the sewing kit that might,
the compass pointing east - or sorth but only works at night.

You find there's always one that works among the coloured duds,
that little squeaking key-ring, that landed in the spuds,
And there it sits on dish so white no problem does it see,
just waiting there to do its job, and lead you to your key.

There's nearly always someone there, an uncle or big brother,
'What sort of battery does it take - it tells you on the cover.'
'It doesn't! - But it must do,' the clever one replied,
'Well let's find out, I'll operate, and take a look inside.'

He reached for knife and fork and spoon, to split the thing in two,
but oh! What a surprise in store as through the air it flew.
The two halves landed locally, but clips and bulb and wire
went flying up into the air - they couldn't have gone higher.

'It's time to eat' the Chef called out, *'It's only a key fob'*
but re-assembled properly, this thing could do its job.
Between each course attempts were made to put the parts in place,
then finally 'twas back again to help the human race.
We're back to moral time again, keep everything adjusted -
But never try to mend it -
'Till it's well and truly busted.

Jim Pritchard

Four Seasons Of Life

Nature imprint's her pattern on life
Spring, summer, autumn and winter's strife
The birth of spring, the joy of life
Bursts forth into summer's dreams
Happy hours, carefree days
Then comes the summer's rains
Alas all too soon
Autumns here, the ebb of life
The seasons have journeyed on.
The chill of winter's icy grip
Claims the weak, the frail, and sick
The span of life is but four season's short.
The clock is wound but once
Each season plays its part.
The hands of time has worked its, hours long
Yet nature's seasons journey on.

Barbara Morrow

Children In Dreams

Unicorns and Dragons
Fairies and Gnomes,
All in a child's imagination
In a dreaam world all of their own.

They ride upon white horses
through the country far and wide.
As knights in shining armour
with swords by their sides.

One rides upon a Unicorn
to a castle in the sky.
With golly his best friend,
and a teddy with one eye.

Three sit on a log,
But it's a magical machine,
taking them to a world of magic
That grown-ups have never seen.

Some played in a forest
just a footsteps from their home
In a bright magical world of Fairy
Elf and Gnome.

Kenneth Mark Alla

The True Christmas Spirit

As I walked through the snow, one Christmas eve night,
It was so, very quiet, there was no one in sight.

But as I turned my head, to look across the street,
This little girl, my eyes did meet.

She was standing by a window, just peering in,
Her little hands were clutching, a biscuit tin.

Her clothes were so ragged, her clothes were so torn,
Shoes with holes, that looked ever so worn.

But this little girl's face, just shone with glee,
As she stood and stared, at a Christmas tree.

Bright lights upon it, like glittering gold,
She forgot that she was standing, outside in the cold.

By a cosy bright fire, children were sitting,
Mothers were chatting, and doing their knitting.

There were sounds of laughter, and sounds of cheer,
Some people dancing, and the men drinking beer.

The fire looked so warm, and really inviting,
The spread on the table, was very enticing.

This poor little girl, made my heart really sink,
But then her happy little face, made me think.

The splendour in life, for granted we take,
Luxury for this little girl, would be, just one piece of cake.

Oh if only it was me who lived in that house, the door would
                                                                    open wide,
I would take her by her little hand, and bring her right inside.

I would let her sit, by that cosy, warm fire,
She could choose from the table, whatever she did desire.

No, I will never forget, that Christmas eve night,
When that little girl's face, was shining so bright.

If only we thought of people like her, when Christmas time is
                                                                    here,
People who have no one in their life, and face everyday with
                                                                        fear.

A little girl holding a biscuit tin, with nothing in it,
To help people like her, would show the true Christmas spirit.

   Christine Bolton-Pearson

Rainbows

The rain falls hard and hits the ground
Thumping the windows with thunderous sound
Hitting the people and cars outside
With only the wind to act as a guide.
Breaking through the wisps of grey
The sun appears with dancing rays
Warming the planet with golden heat
Making a rainbow where sun and rain meet.
Red, orange, yellow and green
Natural beauty there to be seen
Blue, violet and indigo too
I watch the rainbow fade from view.
Angry black clouds swallow the sun
Bringing sorrow and misery to all but one
I watch the clouds move to and fro
And wait again to see rainbows.

Marty Greenwell

Autumn

The warm sunrise pushes the autumn frost away
The world is silent and calm
There is peace in this autumn
Brown crispy leaves scatter from the unseen wind
I am cold but my insides are warm
I am not lonely
Or sad
I am autumn

Jennifer C Taylor

Memories

Christmas cake and Christmas pudding,
Tinsel on the tree,
Sparkling lights and holly berries,
Lovely sights to see,
Snowflakes falling to the ground,
Fluttering with ease,
Snowballs flying through the air,
That catch the winter's breeze.

Carolyn Finch

Leaves

Light filters through with the morning sun
Showing up the hues of the leaves so frail
Bright slashes of crimson red blood
Gentle greens backing them up
Hiding the tiniest wildlife around

Rich warm browns and gentle primrose yellow
All mixed up with some soft sweet pink
Watchful the ladybird tending the plants
As the gaudy purple and black butterfly
Flutters its wings as it flies on its way

Leaves hanging down and leaves standing proud
Some are but strands of gossamer so fine
To cover sweet buds straining to find
The sun shining down helping them grow
Some taking shelter from the chill of the wind

Summer is coming just look for the signs
Listen to the sweet song of the swallows
As they duck and they dive while building a home
For their mate to be safe and produce lots of babes
Before flying once more towards much warmer climes.

Fiona Higgins

Season Of Goodwill

The snow came gently down
All was quiet and still
But then the clock chimed the hour
'Twas the season of goodwill
And in the distance
Choirs of voices sweetly singing
The well loved Christmas Carols
And church bells loudly ringing
To herald the season of goodwill
Gifts all brightly wrapped
Lie beneath the tree
Decorated with stars and tinsel
For the festivities
Upon this season of goodwill
Excitement fun and cheer
When friend visits friend
In a happy atmosphere
In this the season of goodwill
But let us for a while at least
Take a moment to reflect
Of a time many years ago
When a mother and her new born son
A stable had to share
With sheep ox and beast
And angels everywhere
Heralded the season of goodwill

Hazel Smith

Another Year Goes By

Summer's almost over
Winter's at the door
And like the cliffs of Dover
Snow may pave the floor

Nights will be much colder
Days will be so short
And on each burdened shoulder
So heavy is each thought

Log fires maybe burning to melt the frozen sky
But memories keep returning
And another year goes by

The spring will then start calling
With her flowers in full bloom
But tears will keep on falling
Inside each lonely tomb

Lawrence Joseph Sparks

Untitled

Such delights do greet my eye
When I look out into spring
Pink and white like snow falls blossom
The birds above they sing
In the distance stand tall and green
The trees with hills behind
What a sight I've beheld today
It makes life so divine

   M Connor

Autumn

A full moon shines over the distant trees,
The wind whispers soft to the dying leaves,
The earth is rich with harvest's scent,
And the apple tree boughs with fruit are bent.

From the hedgerow comes a rustling sound
Of tiny creatures, close to the ground,
Gathering berries and seeds galore,
Which they quickly add to their winter store.

Do you remember a night like this?
A night that was filled with a heavenly bliss.
When the light of your love made the moon seem dim,
And the wind in the leaves sang a lover's hymn.

Will a night like this ever come again,
Will our harvest always be parting's pain?
Will we ever walk in the full moon's shine
As we harvest a future that's yours and mine?

Valerie J Owen

The Storm

I stand there, snugly, safely, behind my double glazing,
And watch the storm approaching, it really is amazing,
Tiny little lightning flicks, across the sky are dancing,
Thunder grumbles gently, the storm is now advancing.
Heavy hang the storm clouds, like alien udders down,
Blotting out the sunshine, as all the heaven's frown.
Great, blasting bolts of lightning, shoot across the sky,
The thunder's roar is deafening, the storm is coming nigh,
All nature crouches, terrified, 'neath the raging stormy blast,
But sunbeams peep out fitfully, the storm is racing past,
The sun, in all its glory, dominates the earth,
Peace and quiet rule supreme, in glorious new birth.

Nancy Knight

A Happy Wholesome Christmas

A Christmas tree, with twinkling lights,
Lights your homeward journey, shining bright,
A fire in a blazing hearth,
A house that's full of joy and mirth.
You turn the corner, the lights on in the porch,
No need, in the pocket, for a torch.
The light is shining, clear and bright,
A welcoming sight, on a dark stormy night.
The doorbell rings, and the rafters sing,
To the sound of happy laughter,
The turkey's cooked, the children sing,
Of peace, goodwill, ever after.
The Babe in the manger, ah, what of Him,
Carols to Him, we will always ring
Out from the churches, out of the houses,
Out of the farms, even from mouses.
For every creature, and every creed.
Will always at midnight, turn to heed
The spoken word, in the good grave book,
Whose stories need a second look, for,
The First Christmas, will always be with us, and,
It deserves a rousing chorus,
Of carols sung in the old fashioned way, of,
The Star that shone as bright as day,
Which led the shepherds, and showed the way.
And as we eat, and have our fill,
Of meat and vegetables, and a gill, of
Good sweet wine, but toe the line of,
Forgetfulness.
For some, there is no blazing fire, of,
Walking the streets, they do tire.
Other people, of different religions,
Other people, have another Vision of
Christmas, and the New Year.

So let's all celebrate, in our own sweet way,
The Festive season, in our own sweet way of,

Christmas day!
Remember to bake a Christmas Cake,
For lo! It is His birthday we celebrate!
God bless our Christmas bake.

Rosemary Peach

An Autumn Morning

He gives us beauty of the day -
Enlightenment of nature's way
Awakened in the early light
The gentle stir of grass verge life
Lightly pressing earth's fresh yield
Stillness in the rich brown field
Gentle moisture rises there
To greet the morning kiss of air.

Dew drenched webs with sparkled beads
In amongst the textured leaves
Golden fruits and berries bright
Rhythm that reflects His might
Reserves of nature thus portrayed
In bud and briar, in glory blaze.

D Williams

Winter's Wind

Winter's wind blows loud and shrill,
Swaying trees upon the hill,
Bare the boughs, the leaves now shed,
Snow and ice for small boy's sled.

The winds of spring now follow on,
Warmer air, the cold wind's gone,
Then rain comes down and soaks the earth,
To give a start to new year's birth.

Winds of summer, just breezes now,
Green the meadow with the grazing cow,
Gone the thoughts of winds and wet,
The fickle mind can soon forget.

Now quietly comes the summer's sun,
The great outdoors with all its fun,
Only breezes light and warm,
And just perhaps the thunderstorm.

Enjoy these days, for soon they fly,
And the wind once more begins to sigh,
The trees again sway on the hill,
And winter's wind blows loud and shrill.

Katie Hill

The Skies Have It

On a quiet, dew dropped, summer, Somerset and somersaulted day
I wandered among the pink, white and red wild flowers of valerian
That bordered, snuggled up to rills o'er hung by fronds of fern,
Which ran to end in pebble banks, the sea and a single tern
Seen looking upwards to the gilded gorse and the high, fiery,
                                                          heather
And to the occasional intervening ribbed breast of swelling corn,
Amidst the folding brown and green, that did otherwise adorn
The rolling vales, that stared to Wales, to the silvered sea and
                                           brewing weather,
Which like me rejoiced in the stillness and freshness of the day
                                           gathered hay.
But such is the capriciousness of nature and her everyway
That the winner, by far, on this well lightened Quantock day
Was the sky and its mounds of suspended solvent cloud
The 'Bernese Oberland' caught astride the Brendon hills well proud,
With serrated, high, white snowed clouds like mountain spills
And grey, silvered and black puffballs, in sometimes spirals sills
Then banks, serried ranks and tumultuous free falls;
All of overpowering majesty and all imposing beauty idyllic
Never to be quite captured by palettes of oil, water or acrylic
That drew all of one's being upwards to the highest of heavens
Raised like yeast bread, one's least spirits so leavened.
Yes, on that day of strato-orogenesis, the ayes and the skies had
                                                                  it!

D G Viall

Autumn Fairies

See the autumn fairies
Breezing down from high.
Floating on the coloured
Leaves
From trees that reach
The sky.

Fairies dressed in flowing
Voile,
Colours matching golden
Leaves and earth's rich
Soil.

Whilst autumn winds do
Blow this night.
The moon's last rays
Give dancing fairies
Light.

They dance and twirl
In autumn winds,
As moonlight floods
The glen.

But as the day begins
To dawn,
They'll ne'er be seen
Again.

Beryl Smyter

Awakening

Awakening
Suddenly it's spring
The air is full of hope
Love is given another chance
Love helps us all to cope
The winter darkness
Gives way to spring's light
Birds reappear to our delight
Building their nests out of our sight
Daffodils unfurl, gold and serene
The lawns come alife
Enhancing the gold with their green
We are awakened by feelings so bold
Our heads rule our hearts
As we come in from the cold
Not mistaking the pleasure it brings
Spring makes us think of weddings
Brides, honeymoons and rings
The past soon forgotten when we think of
               of these things
Suddenly we are awakened!

Daisy Thompson

An Ode For A Summer Love

'Mmm, it's late summertime, or is it now crispy September?
Anyhow, your crystal clear eyes'll make me remember.
I go, 'golly good gosh', as I visage your face,
And your earrings, and clothes - seriously, they're ace!
If there's a severe lack of sunshine on a rainy day,
Thinking of you'll wash the blues away.'

Mike Achiampong

Winter

It was only just a snowflake
falling slowly from the sky,
but conjured up within the mind
was the question, would it lie.
By now more flakes were flowing
swirling gently in the breeze,
the green grass turned a brilliant white
and the dark night brought a freeze.
As morning broke the snow was thick
a white blanket to behold,
more heavy falls were on the way
so the weather forecasts told.
More snow arrived just as they said
no truer word was spoken,
the snow was heavier than before
electricity power lines broken.
Soon roads were blocked and lorries stuck
they could only sit and wait,
trapped in their cabins for the night
seemed to be their present fate.
More roads were blocked and schools were closed
children told to stay at home,
to pass the time away they could
throw snowballs at the garden gnome.

Stan Tweedie

Kid's Christmas

Christmas tomorrow,
Mum has been baking,
Hiding presents.

Dad will get socks
A frilly pinny for Mum,
What will I get?

Something EE-normous
All kids will want one,
But I'll be the first.

Better be good,
Go to bed early,
Christmas OOH.

Joan Plant

A Summer Corn Field

In a lovely field of corn,
That's a golden yellow,
Sitting there enjoying the view,
A smell of freshness, all around,
Colours, of shear beauty stuns your eyes,
Birds singing, their sweet songs,

Everywhere you look,
Hardly, taking it all in,
The calming effect, it has on you,
With the sun upon your face,
A soft cool breeze, kisses the wheat,

Here is summer at its best,
Nature, in all its glory,
The smells the sound, the sight,
Makes you feel glad to be alive,
Your sensors are reeling,

The day is electric,
How mind expanding, this is,
Nature changers its colours and face,
As the day, starts to fade away,
Slowly falling into the night.

D Godbold

The Battlefield

In fiery fury, the maddened hosts
Thundered on, crazed with the lust to kill.
The light of battle in their eyes.
The stench of blood in their nostrils.
Over the crest of the hill,
Gone forever from our sight.
Lingering, only on the air,
Is the sound of the Last Post.
The red earth marks their resting place.
The air, that such a little time before
Was rent with war cries,
Is silent now, with the majesty of death.
The kindly earth has covered up their shattered bodies
From the common view.
In time, the plough will till the land
And, from the massacre of youth.
Will spring life anew.

Nina du Pille

Forgotten Fleets Reunion (Portsmouth 1995)

As summer's carefree song was yielding
 to early autumn's more measured voice.
A clouding sky and thunder pealing
 would not diminish their hope and choice.

By Solent's edge, ten thousand strong,
 they came to re-live days long gone.
Good times remembered - bad ones suppressed.
 Old friendships nurtured - some new ones blest.

How smart the GI's smooth blue serge,
 not like the coarser weave we knew.
How young they looked, as we once were,
 so full of pride, as we were too.

With patient grace and humorous quip,
 they fanned the spark their fathers lit.
Encouraged us to smarter step,
 with Ghurka pace, a waggish threat!

In peaceful times we soon forget,
 how young men filled a nation's needs.
Don't mock these men, nor scorn their pride,
 there was great purpose in their deeds.

Bill Scovell

Untitled

Hid from the garish sun's enquiring eye,
The little stars our comfort, you and I,
Folded in black-browed night's deceitful arm,
Yet knew she still would keep us safe from harm.

We knew, just as Verona's children knew,
Lovers are safe, if but their love be true;
For youth's a charm to conjure cruel fate:
Safe Montague and sheltered Capulet.

O Romeo, Romeo, banished far away!
Wherefore thy star-led vessel tempest-tossed?
Juliet's bright eyes closed to the light of day:
Too soon they saw their love, like ours, star-crossed!

    B Manfredi

Weather Forecast

Pitter patter, pitter patter,
Here comes rain
Falling on the windowsill
Falling on the pane
What I want is sleep now,
What I want is peace
What I want is quietude
And God's good grace

Flurry flurry, Flurry flurry,
Here comes snow
Falling on the highborn,
Falling on the low,
What I want is rest now
From the world's travail
What I want is your love, Lord,
To which I may avail

No sound I hear, but spring sunshine
Does beat upon my home
Shining on the grass anew
Shining from his throne
Showing us the way it is
Just why he sent His Son
The rain, the snow, the sunlight
But most of all - His Son

Philip Tyler

Impatience

The Motorist! The most impatient 'man' in the world
Cause him to slow down and he'll give you his horn
Cause him to stop and you'll wish you were not born
Where can he be heading with such fury unfurled?

Where is he going, to a Conference or business meeting?
What is it, that cannot wait a second or a minute?
Was there enough time for the journey, when he did begin it?
If not careful, and impatient, it is his fate he will be greeting.

(Substitute the feminine, if you feel you must,
but it is the male driver, who has all the thrust.)

I M Parker

Circle Of Life

The Circle of Life
Comes round too quick,
How beautiful everything looks.
The afternoon, dappled with shadow,
Roams over the hills and nooks.
Ribbons of light dance a merry jig,
Pretty as a picture,
How beautiful everything looks.
Reds, oranges, brown and gold,
The day is coming to a close.
The crunch under my feet,
Tell me, autumn is here to unfold.

Marion Moylan

Last Wolf

Close your eyes and sleep,
Your time has come.
Chased from your land,
Harried, harassed and hounded to hell,
You are the last one.
It was not your fault to be caught in time
With hunger in your belly,
And fire in your eyes.
You came from the ancient world, now gone forever,
You climbed the hills to sing
A lonely song, and no-one hears anymore.
They're all gone now.
In your bones are millennia of enmity with us,
But in the end you became closer than a brother.
It's not fair.
Running you cannot escape being hunted,
And you the hunter.
With your passing you take with you the last refuge,
No more to cross the wild land.
We are never the same without you.

Stuart Grant

The Immigrant

Away in a distant and foreign abode
A fair Irish Colleen
Whose dreams are of home
In a city skyscraper no sun shall she see.
Not even a bird song, just to ring in the spring
Loud hooting and braking.
So much traffic not peace
The bustle of all to accumulate
In bright dreams of the night time
The night turns to day
For she's back home once more
On Eireans green isle
Racing through green fields
O'er hill and then dale
With a fresh gentle breeze
She mounts a steep hill
And there in the valley a shrahaune flows clear
Merely tilted the pail filling up to the brim
While then to proceed up a pathway so neat
To a sweet tiny cottage roofed in gold oaten straw
But just as she knocks on the door with delight
'Twas no more than a dream
Of heartfelt love
For my homeland so dear.

Margaret Mary Hurley

Phenomenon

Clouds amass in ebony groups
Bleak armadas. Heavenly troops
Heaving, weaving - a sea of rage
Thor, he snarls - from his cage
Thunders whip cracks the sky
A blinding flash comes back the reply
Thunder grumbles, moans and groans
Windows rattle. Madness roams
Silence falsely soothes the storm
As lightning bolts are born.

Blazing, raging - jagged spears
Strike at will, it nothing fears
Smite and pummel earth and sky
As thunder roars on high.
Storm winds heighten, argue - brawl
Rowdy winds begin to maul
Twist and coil in boisterous plumes
As havoc cruelly looms.
Thunder barks - screams and roars
Light bites back with savage jaws
Rumbles howl, cry and mourn
Light attacks with sneering scorn
Relentless shafts lambast the sky
Thunder heaves, to weak to cry.
Sensing victory, light assaults
Ceaseless barbs strike like bolts
Thrash and rout just one more time
Just one more time to dine.
Thunder's frenzy, whines - declines
Light now tires, no longer blinds
Rumbles fade so clouds withdraw
To smite some other shore.

P Ashby

Garden Of Delight
(For Tracey)

Her garden today is a beautiful place
Warmth from the smile on her radiant face
Honeysuckle scent on fine porcelain form
Peach blossom purity at the gates of dawn
Fountains of light arc above her head
Upon carpets of Dianthus she delicately treads
With innocence and truth she lays her soul bare
Rainbow highlights shine in her dark flowing hair.

Traversing the bluebell wood in her youth
Along the path of her destiny, seeking the truth
Hazily mysterious, Wistaria, vision of blue
Scent of special flowers encircling you
The eternal river flows from her body sublime
Tender dalliance in green pastures of summertime
Rose scented petals are tenderly spread
In deepening crimson, passionate red.

Would she offer an apple from the tree?
If I fell for her, would she fall for me?
Cherish each other and the garden eternally?
Higher consciousness reached, our bodies entwine
Her ethereal soul gently merging with mine
Luminosity vibrating in Eden sunshine.

Jon Wilde